"Told with delicate sensitivity, *The Sky Fox* is a profoundly relatable story about the magic of the imagination and the infinite comfort that can be found in the natural world, when we look close enough. Through the use of colourful, vibrant imagery, illustrating the beauty that surrounds us, Pia and Sarah take us on an unforgettable journey."

– Melanie Hering, *Community Arts Facilitator*

"*The Sky Fox* is a beautiful story, sensitive and gentle, with wonderful illustrations. It guides us through a reconnection with our instinctual selves, so we can feel part of the world."

– Molly Wolfe, *Art Psychotherapist, Sandplay Specialist*

"Learning to be calm and 'in the moment' when experiencing difficult feelings such as loneliness, sadness, worry or fear is a really important core life skill that helps us cope with everyday ups and downs as well as with more stressful situations. This set of three therapeutic fairy stories cleverly explains how we can learn to do this through connecting with nature. A truly wonderful set of resources – of value to us all and in particular to those with emotional or mental health difficulties."

– Sarah Temple, *GP and author, www.allemotionsareok.co.uk*

T0056264

The Sky Fox

This beautifully illustrated and sensitive fairy tale has been created for children experiencing feelings of loneliness and social isolation. With engaging and gentle illustrations to help prompt conversation, it tells the story of a young girl encouraged by an animal-guide to feel more confident in herself, using nature as a support. This book is available to buy as part of the *Therapeutic Fairy Tales, Volume 2* set, which includes *The Waves* and *Into The Forest*.

*Therapeutic Fairy Tales Volume 1 (*2021*)* and *Volume 2* are both a series of short, modern tales dedicated to exploring challenging feelings and life situations that might be faced by young children. Each fairy tale is designed to be used by parents, caregivers and professionals as they use stories therapeutically to support children's mental and emotional health.

Other books in the series include:

- *The Waves: For Children Living With OCD*
- *Into The Forest: For Children With Feelings Of Anxiety*
- *The Night Crossing: A Lullaby For Children On Life's Last Journey*
- *The Storm: For Children Growing Through Parents' Separation*
- *The Island: For Children With A Parent Living With Depression*
- *Storybook Manual: An Introduction To Working With Storybooks Therapeutically And Creatively*

The Sky Fox – part of the *Therapeutic Fairy Tales* series – is born out of a creative collaboration between Pia Jones and Sarah Pimenta.

Pia Jones is an author, workshop facilitator and UKCP integrative arts psychotherapist, who trained at The Institute for Arts in Therapy & Education. Pia has worked with children and adults in a variety of school, health and community settings. Core to her practice is using arts and story as support during times of loss, transition and change, giving a TEDx talk on the subject. She was Story Director on artgym's award-winning film documentary, 'The Moving Theatre,' where puppetry brought to life real stories of people's migrations. Pia also designed the 'Sometimes I Feel' story cards, a Speechmark therapeutic resource to support children with their feelings. www.silverowlartstherapy.com.

Sarah Pimenta is an experienced artist, workshop facilitator and lecturer in creativity. Her specialist art form is print-making, and her creative practice has brought texture, colour and emotion into a variety of environments, both in the UK and abroad. Sarah has over 20 years' experience of designing and delivering creative, high-quality art workshops in over 250 schools, diverse communities and public venues, including the British Library, V&A, NESTA, Oval House and many charities. Her work is often described as art with therapeutic intent, and she is skilled in working with adults and children who have access issues and complex needs. Sarah is known as Social Fabric: www.social-fabric.co.uk.

Both Pia and Sarah hope these *Therapeutic Fairy Tales* can introduce the theme of nature as a resource, alongside art and storytelling, to children and families.

Therapeutic Fairy Tales

Pia Jones and Sarah Pimenta

This unique therapeutic book series includes a range of beautifully illustrated and sensitively written fairy tales to support children experiencing challenging feelings and life situations, as well as a manual designed to support the therapeutic use of story.

Titles in the series include:
Storybook Manual: Working With Storybooks Therapeutically And Creatively
pb: 978-0-367-49117-8 / 2021

The Night Crossing: A Lullaby For Children On Life's Last Journey
pb: 978-0-367-49120-8 / 2021

The Island: For Children With A Parent Living With Depression
pb: 978-0-367-49198-7/ 2021

The Storm: For Children Growing Through Parents' Separation
pb: 978-0-367-49196-3 / 2021

Into the Forest: For Children With Feelings Of Anxiety
pb: 978-1-032-44927-2 / 2023

The Waves: For Children Living With OCD
pb: 978-1-032-44925-8 / 2023

The Sky Fox: For Children With Feelings Of Loneliness
pb: 978-1-032-44922-7 / 2023

These books are also available to purchase in sets:
Therapeutic Fairy Tales
pb: 978-0-367-25108-6 / 2021

Therapeutic Fairy Tales, Volume 2
pb: 978-1-032-11955-7 / 2023

The Sky Fox

For Children With Feelings Of Loneliness

Pia Jones and Sarah Pimenta

Designed cover image: Sarah Pimenta

First published 2023
by Routledge
4 Park Square, Milton Park, Abingdon, Oxon OX14 4RN

and by Routledge
605 Third Avenue, New York, NY 10158

Routledge is an imprint of the Taylor & Francis Group, an informa business

British Library Cataloguing-in-Publication Data
A catalogue record for this book is available from the British Library

Library of Congress Cataloging-in-Publication Data
Names: Jones, Pia, author. | Pimenta, Sarah, illustrator.
Title: The sky fox : for children with feelings of loneliness / Pia Jones
  and Sarah Pimenta.
Description: Mllton Park, Abingdon, Oxon ; New York : Routledge, 2023. |
  Series: Therapeutic fairy tales ; 6 | Audience: Ages 3-8. | Audience:
  Grades 2-3. | Summary: A reassuring fox shows a lonely girl how
  connecting with nature can help her gain self-confidence. Includes a
  note on how to use the book as a therapeutic resource.
Identifiers: LCCN 2022051823 (print) | LCCN 2022051824 (ebook) | ISBN
  9781032449227 (paperback) | ISBN 9781003374534 (ebook)
Subjects: CYAC: Loneliness--Fiction. | Self-confidence--Fiction. |
  Foxes--Fiction. | Nature--Effect of human beings on--Fiction. | LCGFT:
  Picture books.
Classification: LCC PZ7.1.J726 Sk 2023 (print) | LCC PZ7.1.J726 (ebook) |
  DDC [E]--dc23
LC record available at https://lccn.loc.gov/2022051823
LC ebook record available at https://lccn.loc.gov/2022051824

ISBN: 978-1-032-44922-7 (pbk)
ISBN: 978-1-003-37453-4 (ebk)

DOI: 10.4324/9781003374534

Typeset in Calibri
by Deanta Global Publishing Services, Chennai, India

Printed in the UK by Severn, Gloucester on responsibly sourced paper

Acknowledgements

A special thank you to Stuart Lynch for all the time and creative support he generously gave to *The Sky Fox*. A huge thanks also to Tamsin Cooke, Caroline Bailey, Antonella Mancini and Katrina Hillkirk for their insights on first readings. Thanks also to our families and friends for putting up with our absences so patiently while we worked on this series of books.

Thanks also to all the children and adults we have worked with across the years who have helped inspire us.

Thanks to the Speechmark team for all their support of our stories and turning them into such beautiful books. A special mention must go to Clare Ashworth, for her enthusiasm and creative guidance. Her eagle eye came in handy too! And to Molly Kavanagh, Cathy Henderson and Alison Jones for taking our books into production with such care and attention. Our stories always felt in very safe hands.

Hello there,

Thank you for choosing to read our therapeutic fairy tale, *The Sky Fox*, created to help children and families explore feelings of loneliness and isolation, as well as give ideas for support.

Loneliness is not always an easy subject to talk about. It can take many different forms. Sometimes it creeps up on us. Sometimes it takes over. We can also feel that loneliness isn't possible if we are surrounded by people. Yet, that often is not the case.

We hope that *The Sky Fox* opens opportunities to have conversations about the loneliness we can all feel, and that our characters' journeys can offer support for your own experiences.

Warmest wishes,

Pia & Sarah

Once upon a time, there was a Girl who lived with her family in a city, where towers stood tall and bright lights lit the sky. The streets crackled with energy as people bustled about by foot, bus and bike.

From a window, the Girl watched her brother and sister play outside with friends. She sighed, heavy-hearted. *There was no point in joining them,* she already knew. *No-one would pass her the ball.*

In school, it was just the same. She always found herself watching other children. If she tried to speak up, no-one seemed to notice. The Girl wasn't sure when *it* had started, this sense she was in a bubble and didn't quite belong. Even though she felt herself retreating, there was nothing she could do to stop it.

From down the hall, the Girl heard her mother call out;

"Your turn to take out the rubbish, love. And while you're at it, why not go play outside? It's such a nice evening."

"Yes, Mum," she answered, and picked up the rubbish bag to carry outside.

The Girl opened the bin in the street, just as the children circled close-by.

"Can I play?" she asked quietly, dropping the bag inside.

The kids all charged past, unaware, around the corner.

Can they even hear me? thought the Girl.

The Girl slammed the lid of the bin shut. *Bang!* Its loud crash made her jump. Yet... something stirred inside her. *What a great noise*. The Girl lifted the lid and brought it down again, and again.

Just then, she noticed a set of bright eyes staring out from a face of fire-red fur.

"A fox," she gasped, thrilled to see a wild animal so close.

What a beautiful creature! Its glorious tail swished back and forth as if stirring the air.

"Hello there," said the Girl, smiling.

"Good evening," answered the Fox in the most ordinary way. "I love your drumming."

"Oh!" The Girl leapt back in fright. "You can speak."

Shocked, she glanced around her. *Surely this was a prank by her brother and sister!*

"I'm the Sky Fox," went on the creature. "I heard you calling and wondered if you'd like to join me."

"Join you where?" said the Girl, bewildered, checking to see if anyone *was* watching.

"On my dusk patrol," said the Fox. "It won't take long; we're not going far."

"You want *me* to come?" The Girl's eyes shone. "But no-one ever invites me!"

"Even more reason to say yes," said the Fox gently, "so you can connect with your own wild nature and all that lives around you."

"What are you talking about?" said the Girl. "I'm alone in the city. What nature?"

"Tell me…" The Fox paused. "Can you feel your breath going in and out?"

"I suppose so," said the Girl, puzzled.

"Well, that's wild nature at work," said the Fox. "How about taking three slow breaths, one, two, threeeeeee… let it flow through you, in and out like the tide of the sea."

As the Girl did so, to her surprise, her body gave out a shudder of release.

"And how about stamping like a horse?" said the Fox, and the Girl did just that.

Despite feeling a bit silly, she realised how nice it was to feel solid ground beneath her feet.

"Now if you rub your eyes," said the Fox, "take another look around."

As she did so, the Girl blinked. The colours looked different somehow. Even the Fox seemed to have a flurry of sparks around its tail.

"Now follow me," called the Fox, before taking a giant leap and travelling a while before landing.

"You… we… we are flying?" cried the Girl, feeling her own feet lift.

"Just a little bit of help to get us where we need to," said the Fox with a wide smile.

Light as air, they took a giant leap over the wall before landing in another alleyway. The Girl knew this route well. It was her shortcut to school.

"Oh, my goodness," called out the Girl, smiling. "The old tree we always walk by… it's covered in pink popcorn!"

The Girl could not believe it. Here was the tree that she passed every day. It was blossoming with flowers. As the Fox flew towards it, the Girl noticed its leaves laced with tiny veins... like the ones she saw sometimes beneath her skin. Deep inside, she felt a glow.

"Beautiful, isn't it," said the Sky Fox, smiling.

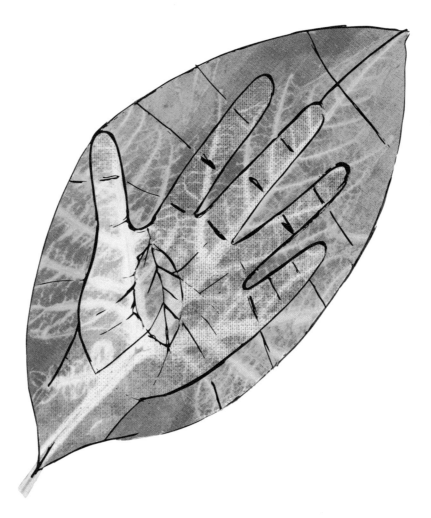

The Girl ran her hands along the bark of the tree and felt her fingertips tingle. The tree's centre felt so solid, ancient and wise. Then, she noticed a spider. About to jump back, she managed to stop herself. The spider was trying to fix its broken web.

"Look how hard it's working," she said in awe, as the spider went about its repairs.

A big bumblebee buzzed past heavy with pollen, while ants marched in a single file, carrying leaves three times their size.

"They are all so little," said the Girl.

"And utterly unique," added the Fox, eyes twinkling. "Each with their own place in the world."

A small bird with a bright orange beak landed on a tree branch. Puffing out its chest, it began to sing. A huge tune from such a tiny creature, it filled the Girl's heart with joy. It was as if she could understand the secret notes... and the bird was singing just for her. Leaning against the tree, the Girl imagined its roots reaching far underground, holding everything in place.

"You know, I've walked past this tree every day," said the Girl to the Fox, "and never paid it any attention. I never knew that the tree could be home to so much life... in the city."

Looking up, she admired how the tree branches seemed to stretch right up to the sky. Under the shelter of the tree, the Girl felt a stillness and a new kind of peace, as if her body were held and supported there.

"Do you see that you are a creature of nature too," added the Fox, "with your own place in the world?"

"Yes." The Girl thought for a moment. "I'm not so alone after all, am I?"

The sun had started to dip, turning the sky purple and light orange. The Girl raised her arms to the sky and saw herself painted in colours. She felt her heart beating, her own pulse of life.

"Thank you," she said, turning to hug the Sky Fox, "for helping me feel all this."

"Never forget you are full of life," whispered the Fox into her ear. "Even more important to *know* it yourself, when people around you don't always seem to."

As they said their goodbyes and the Fox leapt away into the night, the Girl saw her brother and sister back playing with friends. Lowering her head, she was about to slip away unseen.

Only, the Girl remembered how it felt to hear the tiny bird with the impossibly loud song. She saw the spider trying to mend its web, and the ants carrying leaves far beyond their size. She imagined the blossoming tree, rooted and supporting all this life, and felt her feelings rise and a yearning too.

"Hi there," she called to the children, finding her voice. "I'd like to join you. Can I play too?"

Whether they said yes or no, the Girl made sure that she stood up tall and straight. Now she knew how to connect to her own wild nature, inside and around her.

She smiled to herself. *I'm here, with my own place in the world.*

A final word

Did you know that connecting to nature, even in the city, has been proven to help us feel calmer, more grounded and safer inside ourselves? Have you ever had a moment when you've been surprised by finding some hidden corner of nature in the city?

The ancient Japanese tradition, *Shinrin-yoku*, Forest Bathing, of being mindful and present amongst trees (with mobile devices or phones switched off, on silent or put away) has now travelled to many countries. Scientists have proven that trees release invisible chemicals, called phytoncides (wood essential oils), that boost our health and immune system, relaxation and well-being. That wonderful smell of pine trees is actually doing wonders for our body! Equally, evidence shows that chemicals in the earth and soil are also having a calming effect on our body. Some people find the sight and sound of water, rivers or seas calming too.

As many of us live in towns and cities, finding a safe corner in nature can work well, just like it did for the Girl in our story. Please make sure that if you do explore any woods, gardens, parks, streams, rivers and seas, you stay safe, that there are trusted people nearby, and/or people know where you have gone. And if you do come across a fox or any other wild animal, don't try to approach it. Observing animals from a safe distance can be equally magical. And if you don't have access to nature, looking at pictures can also help too!

Your teachers and parents/caregivers can find out more about the idea of nature as a support for well-being in our book *Rewilding Children's Imaginations*, which is packed full of creative ideas of how to connect with nature in fun, safe ways, through art making, storytelling and folktales.

We hope that you can find nature a support, be it a small corner or large spaces.

Pia & Sarah

Therapeutic Fairy Tales Volume 2:

Therapeutic Fairy Tales Volume 1:

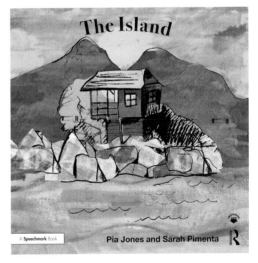